Note to parents

A baby's first encounter with the outside world is
an exciting time for both parent and child. Aimed
at the very young, this book introduces some of
the objects and activities your child will discover
in his or her first few years. Share this book with
your child, pointing to the pictures, naming the
objects and perhaps later encouraging him or
her to repeat the names. Above all, enjoy the
book together.

baby's first picture book

words by Nina Filipek
illustrated by Pamela Venus

Copyright © 1991 by World International Publishing Limited.
All rights reserved.
Published in Great Britain by World International Publishing Limited,
An Egmont Company, Egmont House, P.O.Box 111,
Great Ducie Street, Manchester M60 3BL.
Printed in DDR. ISBN 0 7498 0086 0

A CIP catalogue record for this book is available from the British Library

baby

socks

vest

bib

spoon

dish

panda

train

ball

buggy

coat

shoes

highchair

banana

biscuit

mummy

smile

daddy

walk

trolley

hello

bricks

keys

bath

soap

duck

towel

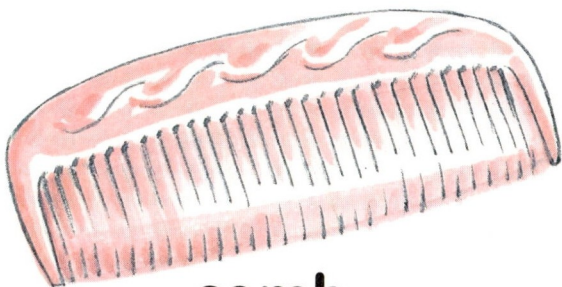

comb

toothbrush

pyjamas

teddy

book

sleep

light

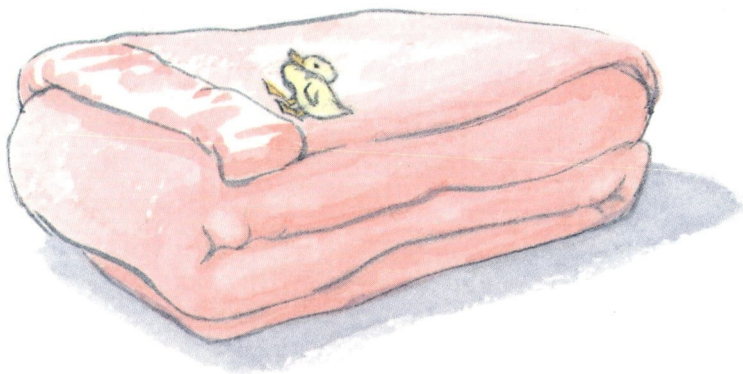

blanket